Splits Method

The Ultimate Beginner's Splits Stretching Flexibility Guide - Safe & Easy Splits Exercises Guide to Stretch Painlessly (No Machines, Cables or Equipment Needed)

By *Freddie Masterson*

For more great books visit:

HMWPublishing.com

Download another book for Free

I want to thank you for purchasing this book and offer you another book (just as long and valuable as this book), "Health & Fitness Mistakes You Don't Know You're Making", completely free.

Visit the link below to signup and receive it:

www.hmwpublishing.com/gift

In this book, I will break down the most common health & fitness mistakes, you are probably committing right now, and I will reveal how you can easily get in the best shape of your life!

In addition to this valuable gift, you will also have an opportunity to get our new books for free, enter giveaways, and receive other valuable emails from me. Again, visit the link to sign up:

www.hmwpublishing.com/gift

Table Of Contents

Introduction	**8**
Definition of the splits:	**15**
Here's a brief list of the different types of splits you can perform:	18
Chapter 2 - Isometric Exercises	**20**
My personal experience with isometric exercises	22
What is proper technique?	23
Chapter 3 - Always Warm Up First	**26**
Why do you need to warm up?	**27**
It's important to know the limits of warm-up exercises.	28
What happens if you forget or don't stretch?	30
Chapter 4 - Test Your Potential	**32**
Step 1): Be sure to warm up and stretch your body.	33
Step 2): Now that you have appropriately positioned your body.	34
Step 3: Now look at the mirror.	34
What have you done?	35
Chapter 5 -Stretching Exercises	**37**
What is Dynamic Stretching?	**38**
Here's some simple fixtures required for stretching exercises:	40
A few benefits of stretching:	41
Precautions during Stretching Exercise (Read carefully):	43

Here's important Stretching Exercises relevant to perform Side Splits: 46

  (1)   Downward Facing Frog: 46
  (2)   Seated Straddle Stretch: 51
  (3)   Butterfly Stretch: 53
  (4)   Hip Adductor Stretch: 55
  (5) Bent leg calf stretch   57
  (6)Front of calf and toe stretch: 59
  A great tip you should keep in mind while stretching   60

Chapter 6 - Stretching: Preparation to do Splits 62

  Reminder for "Preparation-Exercises" before Splits: 63
  Golden-4-Step Freehand – Step - 1:   65
  Golden-4-Step Freehand – Step - 2:   67
  Golden-4-Step Freehand – Step - 3:   68
  Golden-4-Step Freehand – Final Step: 70

Chapter 7 - Simple Stretch For Side Splits 73

Here is another small caution for you: 74
Steps for Simple Stretch for side splits: 74
  Step 1): Starting position for a Side Split: 75
  Step 2): Beginning to get a Side Split   76
  Step – 3: Side Split with Feet pointing up: 77
Benchmark indicator   79

Chapter 8 - Advance Stretches For Full Splits 85

  Posture – 1   86
  Posture – 2   88
  Posture – 3   90

Posture – 4	92
Posture – 5	94
Posture – 6	96
Posture – Perfect	98

Chapter 9 - Tips for 180 - Degree "Side Splits". 99

The Ultimate "7 Steps DAILY Stretching Exercises" to realize your goal of 180 Degree Side Splits 100

Chapter 10 - Contract & Relax   104

What happens when you stretch?   104

- Step 1) Start your CR Training with the Horse Stance Position.   106
- Step 2) Gradually increase the stress on your muscles.   108
- Step 3) When you feel the first slight of stress, do this!   109
- Step 4) Deeper Stretches   111
- Let us summarize the 4 Steps: 112

RECOVERY TIME: 113

- Step 5) Complete a stretching session.   114
- Step 6) Last Intense Contraction.   114

Know the following truth about Relaxed Stretches: 117

Chapter 11 - Practice Splits Every Day   120

Practice the splits daily to see improvement 121

Chapter 12 - Leg Stretches   125

What should be your goal be while performing Leg Stretches?   126

Basic Leg Stretches Exercise   126

Leg Stretches for the Hamstrings: 128
Leg Stretches for the Quadriceps: 133
The Side-lying Version: 135
How to Improve Your Flexibility Safety During Splits. 138

Bonus Chapter: Video Stretching Tutorial 139

Final Words 141

About the Co-Author 144

Introduction

I want to thank you and congratulate you for purchasing this book, "Splits Method". I'm glad to be able to share some ideas and secrets with you today that will help you achieve the dream of performing the perfect splits! Yes, this is something millions of eyes share in common. Let me tell you that the efforts by the majority have proven out to be a wild goose chase since most of the methods being practiced around the world today would burn your sweat, make you fatigued and grant you everything other than your dream of the "PERFECT SPLITS."

My methodology and the main purpose of this short but resourceful book is to make your body HEALTHY and FLEXIBLE in a dramatically uncomplicated and efficient way. I won't stretch this guide and bore you with all the literary talk and complicated discussions, so all the readers out there put a smile on your face because this book is concise yet it has everything that you need to know to convert yourself into becoming a perfectionist in performing the splits. So you must be asking yourself: "Even if this book is an ideal one, what can be the minimum time it will take me to achieve the splits?". The answer to that question is it really depends. It can take as little as a few days to a few months; it all really depends on your current flexibility level.

Moreover, my name is Freddie Masterson and I am the lead author of this book. Before writing this book, I have practiced this stretching technique for over the past TWENTY-FIVE YEARS. If you have tried to perform the splits for a while now and have been stretching regularly. This guide may even help you achieve it in as little time as a few days. You know your body more than anyone else and without any doubt, every person has a unique structure, so the time varies for every single person out there.

As far as what I have done my whole life, I consider this technique to be the BEST because, I have an in-depth experience of yoga, stretching exercises, stretching aiders. I've even bought leg-stretching machines worth 250$, so that I can attain the perfect splits. In a nutshell, I've tried every available option to accomplish the splits, but for me, nothing except this technique worked. I've achieved the best results using this method, and I have demonstrated this technique plenty of times in my martial arts classes.

Thanks again for purchasing this book, I hope you enjoy it.

Also, before you get started, I recommend you [joining our email newsletter](#) to receive updates on any upcoming new book releases or promotions. You can sign-up for free, and as a bonus, you will receive a free gift. Our "*Health & Fitness Mistakes You Don't Know You're Making*" book! This book has been written to demystify, expose the top do's and don'ts and to finally equip you with the information you need to get in the best shape of your life. Due to the overwhelming amount of mis-information and lies told by magazines and self-proclaimed "gurus", it's becoming harder and harder to get reliable information to get in shape. As opposed to having to go through dozens of biased, unreliable and un-trustworthy sources to get your health & fitness information. Everything you need to help you has been broken down in this book for you to easily follow and to immediately get results to achieve your desired fitness goals in the shortest amount of time.

Once again, to join our free email newsletter and to receive a free copy of this valuable book, please visit the link and signup now:

www.hmwpublishing.com/gift

Chapter 1 – Learning The Basics

It is important to learn the basics of SPLITS before we begin this undertaking.

Definition of the splits:

The split is the typical position of the body in which your legs are extended to their utmost but in opposed directions. Look at the picture below to visualize the side splits.

While performing the split the angle between the two legs is almost 180 degrees. Let's learn a little more about the basics of splits:

A split exercise involves the astonishing flexibility of three muscles: Iliacus – Psoas – Hamstrings

- **Iliacus** - As per Wikipedia - The iliacus is a flat, triangular muscle, which fills the iliac fossa on the interior side of the hipbone.

- **Psoas** - Psoas is a surface muscle, which most of us can't flex or release at will. It is s deep tissue involved in complex moves and interactions through the core and lower part of the body.

- **Hamstrings** - The Hamstrings muscles is comprised of three separate muscles, the Biceps, Femoris, and Semitendinosus. They are primarily fast-twitch muscles, responding to low reps and powerful movements.

A thorough knowledge of muscles is essential, but it is not mandatory to become an expert while we learn more about the splits. Splits can also be classified into a variety of types by the body orientation.

Here's a brief list of the different types of splits you can perform:

- Side Splits
- Over Splits
- Front Splits
- Vertical Splits
- Twisting Splits
- Half Splits
- Straddle Split Leap

Once you learn to do the side splits all the other kinds of splits come along very smoothly and without that much more effort. Side splits is the type of splits in which both legs are in the opposite direction concerning the trunk. You can scroll back to see the picture of Side Splits. We will now step into the core of the subject – "ISOMETRICS" – the prime requirement for achieving the splits.

Chapter 2 - Isometric Exercises

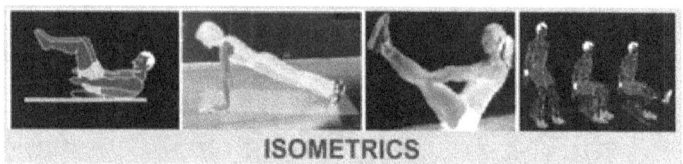

We are slowly entering into the arena to perform actual side splits. If you have ever tried to do side splits, you should know the importance of muscle strength to perform it without pain. When your muscles are in firm position, you'll be putting a lot of command on your muscles. That command includes your WEIGHT and ISOMETRIC CONTRACTION.

Isometrics are a type of exercise training in which the Joint Angle and Muscle Length do not change during contraction. Isometrics is in contrast to concentric or eccentric contraction, which is typically called dynamic or isotonic movements. Isometrics is done in static positions, rather than being dynamic through a range of motion. Look at the figures above, and you will began to understand what are isometrics exercises.

Isometric contraction is a POWERFUL, EXTREME and MEANINGFUL contraction of the muscles that increase the length, force, and elasticity necessary for splits. You are doing this type of exercise style in order to FATIGUE your body rather than putting it in PAIN because fatigue is the main hindrance between you and perfect side-splits. Eventually, when you keep doing the isometric exercises, it will fatigue your muscles even more and leave them nothing but RELAXED, and this is what we want to accomplish.

My personal experience with isometric exercises

While I was in the Brazilian Jiu Jitsu demonstrations, our instructor made us undergo accurate control, weight and fatigue management. However, if our instructor caught us using our muscles or what I like to call "muscling methods." (Muscling is the utter dependence on muscle strength during grappling), he would have us go off to the side and do 50 push-ups. He would do this over and over again until our arms were so fatigued; we were incapable of "muscling" the techniques... even if we tried!

Muscling is NOT of prime importance because if you rely only on muscle strength the moment your muscles get fatigued you will surrender. Furthermore, by having our muscles so fatigued, we were forced to use leverage and proper technique!

What is proper technique?

This is what we call "isometrics." It protects our muscles against injury. The resistance of the three muscles is what makes the splits so difficult to attain. Striving hard to accomplish side splits but our hopes shattered, we start looking for MIRACLES.

We buy expensive stretching machines worth almost $250.00 and expect that agonizing ourselves will lead to any betterment in our progress with the side splits, which could cause permanent detriment to your muscles. I don't want to be sarcastic at all but this is what almost every one of us did including ME, and we failed poorly.

Isometrics on the other hand, repairs the muscles the same way as weight training. Isometrics makes the muscles stronger, more flexible, and ELONGATES them. We will proceed to SIDE SPLIS now. However, before we do that, it's necessary to summarize the key points of the above paragraphs.

- Isometric is a type of exercise training in which the joint angle and muscle length do not change during contraction.

- If you keep doing isometric exercises, it will fatigue your muscles even more and leave them nothing but RELAXED, and this is the primary requirement of achieving the side splits

Chapter 3 - Always Warm Up First

> *"To improve range of motion and avoid injury, you do need to stretch, but don't ever do it when muscles are cold." - William Levine, MD, Orthopedics surgeon and director of sports medicine at Columbia University Medical Center in New York City.*

You must start your warm up with some light aerobic free hand exercises to get the blood to your muscle tissue and before doing any stretching.

Why do you need to warm up?

Warm-up exercises are crucial before you do any workouts, or try to qualify for the above test - "Test your Potential." Preparing the muscles and joints for more intense activity will prevent injury, and promote blood circulation. Warm-up exercises increase the temperature of the body and make the muscles more flexible and receptive to strenuous activity. An overwhelming number of experts will agree that you should first do warm-up exercises before stretching. Warming up should increase your heart rate but not to the level experienced during actual SPLITS.

Do the usual exercises that you do to warm and loosen up your muscles. Start from simple jogging to stretching. WARM UP your body to let your muscles relax especially the hamstrings and iliopsoas. These can specifically be termed as the "Muscles of the back of the thigh."

It's important to know the limits of warm-up exercises.

You must listen to your body. If you are feeling tired, uncomfortable or notice a decrease in performance, you may need more recovery time or a break from warm-up altogether. If you are feeling active, you do not force yourself to do the exercises slowly.

If you pay attention, your body will let you know what it needs and when it needs to stop.

If you feel tired, it is better to do brisk walking or slow jogging for about ten to fifteen minutes, rather than stretching before exercise. The meaning of cooling down simply means slowing down, and never stopping altogether. Continuing to move around at a very low intensity for 5 to 10 minutes after a workout helps remove lactic acid from your muscles and may it will also contribute to reducing muscle stiffness.

What happens if you forget or don't stretch?

If by chance you forget to warm up your body, you will or could eventually damage your muscles, cause pain, and surely will not be able to do splits. Remember, the fatigue from the vigorous workout will allow your muscles to relax. A good warm-up prepares your body for more intense activity.

Warming up will allow your body time to adjust to the demands of exercise.

You should warm up for 5-10 minutes by doing some light exercises as outlined in the following chapter and **then** you should stretch. The reason for this is that stretching cold muscles can directly contribute to pulled and torn muscles.

Stretching, or should I say dynamic stretching will help your body to get ready for training. It's also an essential part of recovering from a warm-up activity. Again, you should switch to stretching after warm up and all training sessions should also end with stretching.

Chapter 4 - Test Your Potential

You must test your potential before you try to attempt a side splits. There are a few things that this book can't teach you, and testing your potential for the side splits is one of them. You need to do it yourself, as it is a self-evaluation process.

Your PELVIS is the only hurdle between you and you achieving the perfect side splits, unless you have some physical deformity. However, you should not worry, practice makes everyone perfect. Also, before you build up too much anxiety because of this test, let me relieve your tension. In my entire career, I have never seen anyone FAIL this test. We'll experiment the bony structure by performing HALF SIDE SPLITS.

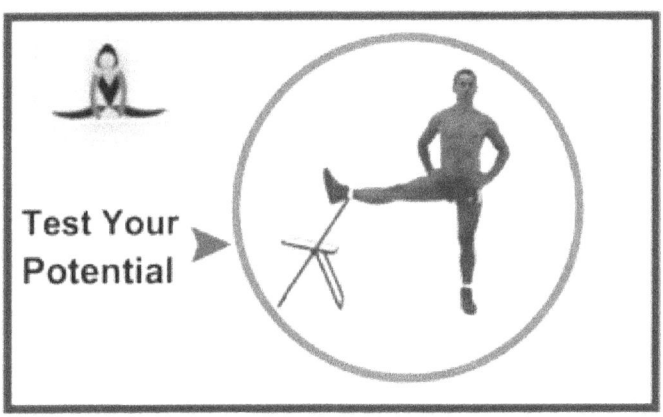

Step 1): Be sure to warm up and stretch your body.

Then position your body in such a way that your foot rests on a plane, such the height of plane equals your waist's height, e.g., on an Iron chair, a sofa, a table, a kitchen counter or some gadgets that suits you. It's also best to perform this in front of a mirror.

Step 2): Now that you have appropriately positioned your body. It should look exactly as shown in the picture above. This is a half side splits because your leg is at the right angle concerning your pelvis and is positioned away from the body.

Step 3: Now look at the mirror. Observe if your stance is erect and upright as if your feet are resting on the ground with an upright body. At this point, your hips MUST BE ALIGNED, if you don't acknowledge a "BONE TO BONE" sensation it means you do have the potential for side splits. It is this bone-to-bone sensation that hinders the body to stand in an erect posture.

What have you done?

Yes, you have done "Half Side Splits" with both your legs. This is proof that your hip joints have all the necessary mobility to perform a full side split. You have also proved that both leg muscles are long enough to perform a side splits.

Now you can perform a side splits with both legs stretched sideways simultaneously.

Nothing other than your nervous system will detract you to do a perfect side splits. It's important to teach your nervous system the perfect stretching methods. Once you do this, you will be able to do side splits anytime. I'm confident that very soon you will be the one smiling while doing the side splits! Going forward, please follow this systematic guide without any preconception, as this will help you gain momentum and allow you to progress faster.

Chapter 5 -Stretching Exercises

As we mentioned earlier, you should also switch to stretching after warm up. This will improve your ability to perform side splits. Once your muscles are warm, spend a few minutes on stretching. Since the goal of your warm-up is to increase your heart rate and get ready for a more intense job of side splits, you can choose a stretch that suits your body and workout environment.

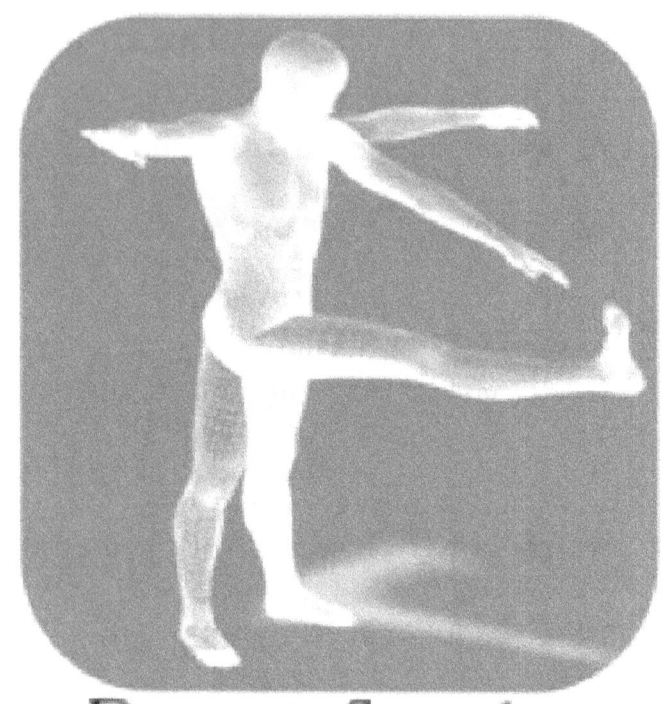

Dynamic Stretching

What is Dynamic Stretching?

Dynamic stretching means slow and controlled movements. It may include simple movements like arm circles, hip rotations, yoga-type movements, and some form of jogging or walking. The three pictures below highlights some postures of different stretches.

Here's some simple fixtures required for stretching exercises:

- Floor mat or carpet for comfortable sitting.

- Table or similar furniture to support your body weight initially.

- Shoes - wearing shoes is suitable for beginners.

- Stopwatch to measure your performance.

Stretching is the key element to help lengthen and loosen your muscles. Stretching is not the first thing you should do before exercising. I'm purposely repeating myself, however I cannot stress this enough. You should always warm up for 5-10 minutes by doing some light exercises and **then** you should stretch. The reason for this is that stretching cold muscles can directly contribute to pulled and torn muscles.

I'll show you the simple methods to perform some select Stretching Exercises relevant to Side Splits. However, before we do that, let me just highlight a few important points of stretching.

A few benefits of stretching:

- Reduces muscle soreness after warm up.

- Accelerates muscle tissue healing

- Improves balance and coordination

- Improves posture

- Promotes muscle relaxation

- Boosts your bodies energy levels

- Relieves back and joint pain

- Reduces the likelihood of back pain

- Promotes total body relaxation and a greater sense of well-being

- Maintains lifelong flexibility

Performing side splits is a challenging operation. This is highly useful for gymnasts, dancers, and for practically any sportspersons. It requires an enormous amount of flexibility in the hamstrings, groin, hip adductors and lower back. Whether you are already flexible or not you will find greater flexibility and range of motion if you stretch your muscles before and after performing a side splits.

Lastly, right before you get started stretching, I want you to pay very close attention and I want you to thoroughly read the following in order to make sure you avoid any injuries.

Precautions during Stretching Exercise (Read carefully):

- Don't force a joint beyond its normal range of motion as this could potentially lead to instability of the joint.

- Be extra careful if you suffer from osteoporosis or are taking steroids as the risk of fractures is elevated.

- Avoid aggressive stretching of muscles that you have immobilized in a splint or cast. Connective tissues lose their strength some periods of immobilization.

- Stretching needs to progress gradually. In some cases it may take up to several weeks of a stretching program before you see significant results, so don't rush it.

- You should not be experiencing more than some transitory discomfort after a stretching session.

- Any pain that lasts for more than a few days may indicate the presence of inflammation. The famous saying "no pain, no gain" really does not apply here.

- Avoid stretching if you have swollen or edematous muscle tissues, as they are more susceptible to damage.

- Avoid over-stretching if you have any weak muscles.

- Make sure you always continue to breathe during a stretch. Holding your breath can affect your blood pressure.

Here's important Stretching Exercises relevant to perform Side Splits:

(1) Downward Facing Frog:

Downward Facing Frog

Downward Facing Frog is a deep stretching exercise for your groins, your hips, and your lower back. Position yourself on all hands and feet on the floor just like the picture, aligning your wrists under your shoulders and your knees under your hips. Open your knees as wide as possible and line up your ankles with your knees. Point your toes and feet turned out to the sides. Imagine that your legs are frog legs splayed out to either side. Rest on your forearms and drop your torso toward the floor. If you feel too much pressure on your knees, then put folded blankets or pillows before coming into the pose. Stay in the pose for at least 30 seconds to five minutes.

Instructions to perform this stretch:

(a) From Table position, tuck the toes under, press into the hands and begin to lift the hips up towards the ceiling.

(b) Spread the fingers wide apart with the middle finger facing forward, and the install your palms shoulder-width apart. Press the out through the fingers and edges of the hands.

(c) Using straight, however not locked arms, press the hips up and back reaching the chest towards the thighs. Lift yourself up through your tailbone to keep your spine straight and long.

(d) Have your feet are hip's width apart with the toes facing forward. Press your heels on into the floor feeling a stretch in your legs and on the back position of the legs. The legs should also be straight, or you can have a small bend in your knees to keep the back flat.

(e) Let the head and neck hang freely from the shoulders or look up at the belly button.

(f) Hold your breath and do this for at least 4-8 breaths.

(g) To release: bend the knees and lower the hips back to Table position, or come all the way down to child pose.

(2)   Seated Straddle Stretch:

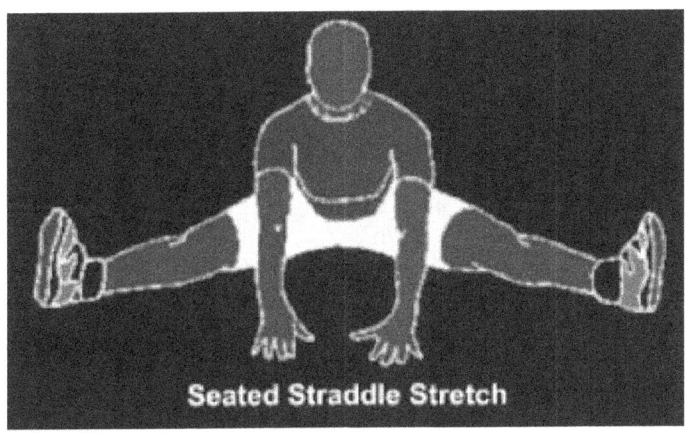
Seated Straddle Stretch

In Seated Straddle Stretch, you will stretch your groin, hamstrings and lower back muscles. Sit on the floor and make sure to keep your spine straight and your legs extended on the floor in front of you. Spread your legs and attempt to put them as wide as possible making a "V" shape, also make sure your knees and toes pointing towards the sky. Engage your core muscles by flexing your belly button inward your spine and lengthen through your spine. Hinge at the waist and fold forward, lower your torso and make sure it is toward the floor. Hold this stretch 30 seconds to 5 minutes.

(3) Butterfly Stretch:

The Butterfly Stretch targets the inner groin, hips and lower back muscles. To perform this stretch, make sure you are sitting up tall with a straight spine. Also make sure to bend your knees, press the soles of your feet together directly in front of your groin. Hold on to your toes with both of your hands. Hinge forward towards your waist and lower your torso as much as possible down toward the floor.

Press the feet into each other firmly to encourage your hips to open up even further. Hold your stretch movement for 30 seconds up to 5 minutes.

(4)   Hip Adductor Stretch:

Sit on a firm surface and place the soles of your feet together forming a circle with your legs. Gently lean forward to feel your inner thigh stretch. For a stronger stretch, use your arms to push your knees gently toward the floor. Hold your position for 15 to 30 seconds. This stretches the hamstring. Repeat this exercise at least 5 times.**Bent leg calf stretch**

(5) Bent leg calf stretch

- Lean against a wall, tree, or chair for support.

- Place your right foot back; make sure to keep your toes pointing forward.

- Slightly bend your left knee, never letting it go beyond your toes.

- Slowly bend your right knee while you are doing this.

- Keep your head up and spine straight.

- Press your heel of the right foot to the ground.

- Hold and then repeat with the left leg.

(6) Front of calf and toe stretch:

- Lean against a wall, tree, or chair for support.

- Bend your left knee and make sure never to let it go beyond your toes.

- Put your right leg back with your toes pointing straight backward.

- Keep your head up and spine straight.

- Gently press the front of the back foot and lower leg toward the floor.

- Hold and then repeat with your left leg

A great tip you should keep in mind while stretching

Stretch your body until it is fatigued. You should not put yourself in pain. If you feel pain, then your body is not sufficiently tired.

Extensive documents are covered in Chapter – 3- "Always warm up first" and here Chapter – 5 – "Stretching Exercises."

Read the chapters carefully, and master theses stretches. Try both the exercises. If you could not pass – Chapter - 4 –"Test your potential" try now, and I'm confident that you will pass the test.

Chapter 6 - Stretching: Preparation to do Splits

Our mission is for me to teach you Splits through this book. You will notice that I have introduced representative images in every chapter. I believe you can do Splits with this guide, but you need to read it several times and practice the exercises by following the images, till you can perform your selected tasks at ease. We're very close to learning the technique of doing Splits. You have to master this chapter because you have to achieve easy stretching to learn the splits.

There are two types of splits, the Side Split, and Front Splits. Both these splits will demand considerable flexibility in your lower back, hamstrings and inner thighs. I've shown you a series of preparatory Stretching Exercises in "Chapter – 5- Stretching Exercises". Before you try to stretch yourself to learn to do the splits, you must attain the required flexibility through stretching exercises. This is the primary requirement for a fruitful and painless Split.

Reminder for "Preparation-Exercises" before Splits:

[?] Warm up with a 10-minute exercise – see – Chapter -4 – "Always warm up first."

- Do "Seated Straddle Stretch- (see Chapter 5)

- Stand with your feet shoulder-width apart and your arms by your side.

- Swing your right leg up and try to touch your thigh to your chest.

- Keep the leg straight throughout the movement and swing your arms to help your balance.

- Do 20 repetitions and then switch legs.

Final Check: Have you achieved considerable flexibility in the lower back, hamstrings and inner thighs? If not, follow this Golden-4-Step Freehand Exercise, and you'll be ready for Splits:

Golden-4-Step Freehand – Step - 1:

- Lie on your back on an exercise mat. Keep your left leg straight and bend your right leg. Lift your right leg and bring your thigh as close as you can toward your chest. Hold the position and count to 10. Cross your bent leg over your straight leg and try to touch your knee to the floor while keeping both shoulders on the floor.

- Hold and count to 10 again.

- Repeat the same sequence of movements with your left leg. Bend both legs, keep them together and lift them toward your chest. Keep your back on the floor.

- Hold and count 10.

- Lower both legs, so your thighs form 90-degrees with your body and your feet are off the floor. Keep your legs together and knees bent and swing them to your left. Try to touch knees to the floor. Hold for 10 seconds and swing to your right.

These exercises will improve the flexibility of your lower back.

Golden-4-Step Freehand – Step - 2:

- Sit on an exercise mat with your back straight.

- Bend both legs and place the soles of your feet together. Get your heels as close to your groin as possible. Grasp an ankle with each hand and rest your elbows on the inside of your thighs. Gently push down on your thighs with your elbows and try to touch your knees to the floor. Hold the position and Count 10. Relax and Repeat five times.

- On the fifth time, lean forward and try to get your chest as near the floor as possible.

- Hold the position for 10 seconds, relax and repeat four more times. This stretches your groin, inner thighs, and lower back.

Golden-4-Step Freehand – Step - 3:

- Sit on a bench or couch.

- Place one foot on the floor and stretch your other leg out on the bench in front of you. Bend the leg on the bench slightly, lean forward and grasp the balls of your foot. Gently pull the balls and toes of your foot toward you until you feel a stretch in your calf.

- Hold and count of 20. Now relax for 2 minutes.

- Next, pull the balls of your foot more firmly toward you and simultaneously try to straighten your leg by pushing against your hand with your calf muscle.

- Do not straighten your leg. Hold and count 20. Relax for 2 minutes. Next, stretch your hamstrings. Straighten your leg, place your hands close to your heel, lean forward and try to touch your chest to your thigh.

- Hold for 20 seconds.

- Change legs and repeat the sequence of movements.

Golden-4-Step Freehand – Final Step:

- Perform the seated stretch.

- Sit on the floor with both legs stretched out to the sides as wide as possible. Lean to the one hand, bend from the hips and try to touch your chest to your knees. Hold for 10 seconds then lean to your other side and repeat the movement.

- Next reach forward with both hands, bend from your hips and try to touch your chest to the floor. Hold and count 10.

Repeat the sequence of movements. This stretches your inner thighs, hamstrings, and hips.

(Note: You may use a partner to help you do the seated stretch. Your partner sits in front of you with their legs spread out wide and leans forward to grip your wrists. He positions each heel on the inside of your feet and gently pushes your legs out wider while pulling you forward).

- Hold the stretch and count 10.

- Relax for 2 minutes and repeat.

- Now you should be ready to do Splits.

Chapter 7 - Simple Stretch For Side Splits

The splits is one of those moves that is easy for some people and much harder for others. Even if you have tight muscles, you will still be able to master it if you work hard and continually stretch.

In this chapter, I will show you simple stretch movements for side splits. It will be wise for a beginner to master the "Simple stretches" first before moving on to "Advanced Full Split Stretches" in the following chapter.

Here is another small caution for you:

Be sure to do each stretch on both sides – you will want a good splits on both your right leg and your left leg. Also, do not perform theses stretches until you feel that you are ready to do so. Practice all the stretches mentioned previously to be as flexible as you can and only then gradually begin the stretches mentioned in this chapter. We want to avoid any injuries at all costs! Please follow the Illustration below.

Steps for Simple Stretch for side splits:

Step 1): Starting position for a Side Split:

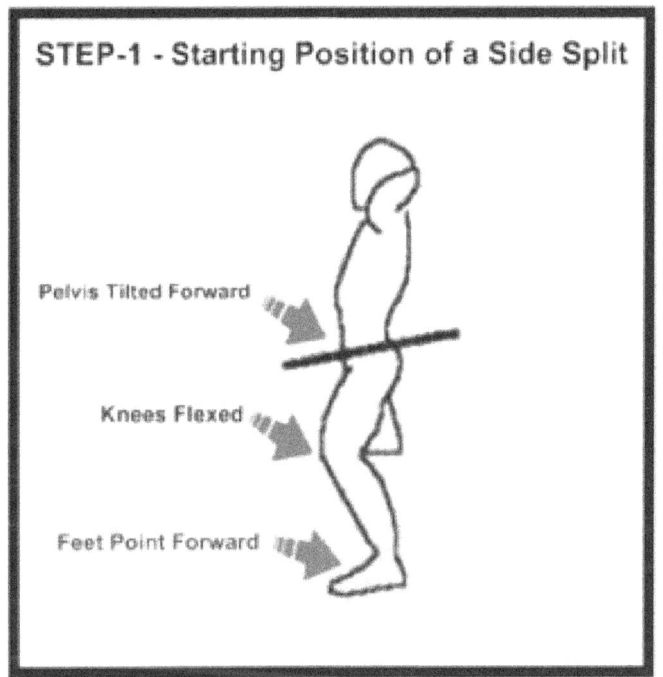

- Make your feet to point forward

- Flex your knees as shown

- Point your feet forward as shown

- Repeat till you can do it at ease

Step 2): Beginning to get a Side Split

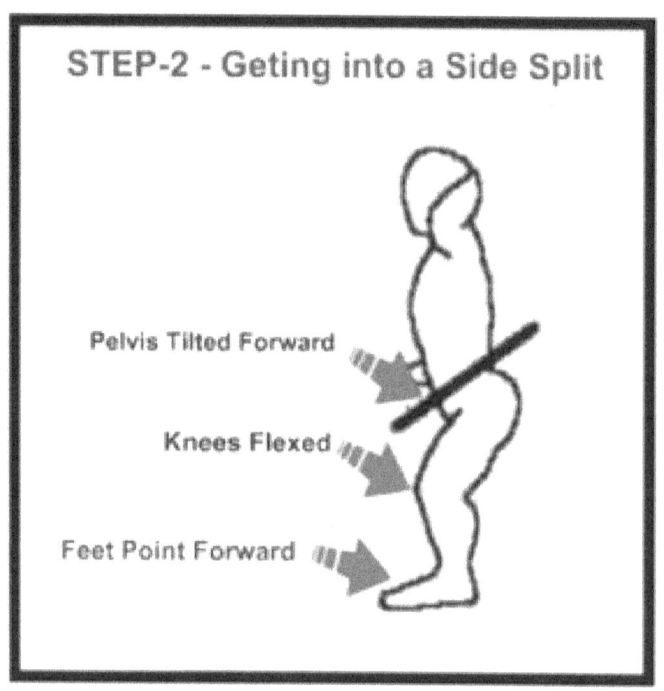

- Spread your Legs sideways

- Tilt your Pelvis more as shown

- Point your feet forward as shown

- Repeat till you can do it at ease

Step – 3: Side Split with Feet pointing up:

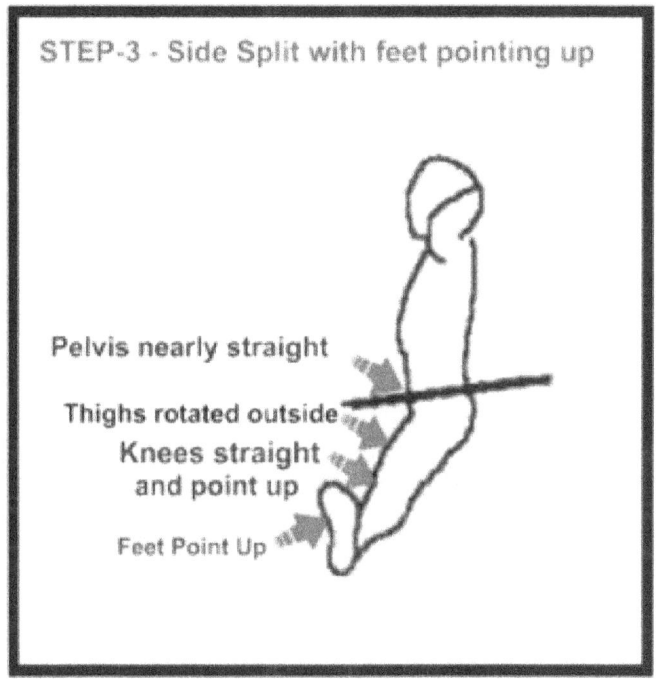

- Make your hips straight

- Make your Pelvis nearly straight as shown

- Make your knees straight and pointing up

- Rotate your thigh outside as shown

- Repeat till you can do it at ease

Benchmark indicator

Now I've created a **Benchmark indicator** for you. Check your "Simple Stretch Side Split" performance after you have trained yourself in the above Three Steps.

(1)   **See the figure below.** O.K! Keep your back upright and your pelvis tilted forward. Hips forward, and do not let you butt sag back on an upright side split stretch. If you can do this accurately, your Benchmark = 2.

(2) **See the figure below** and make your ankles, knees, and hips in a straight line. If you can do this side split position correctly, then your Benchmark=4. Not a bad Benchmark.

(3) Look at the picture below, and maintain the position of your hips right up on the chair with the back upright and ankles, knees, and hips in a straight line. If you can do it easily and keep it for 5 minutes after a few trials, your Benchmark=6.

(4) **See the picture below.** You increase your stretch and relax for at least 2 minutes. If you can do it, your Benchmark=8. Keep it up and proceed to get a perfect 10. Good Luck!

(5) Now, look at the picture below.

This is the final position. If you can remain in this Side Split position for 5 minutes, your Benchmark = 10 = Full Mark. Bravo, this is a great success!

Chapter 8 - Advance Stretches For Full Splits

Once you have achieved 10/10 in the above Simple Stretch for Side Splits, you have to move to Advance Stretches for Full Splits.

Study the Illustration and try to imitate the postures below:

Posture – 1

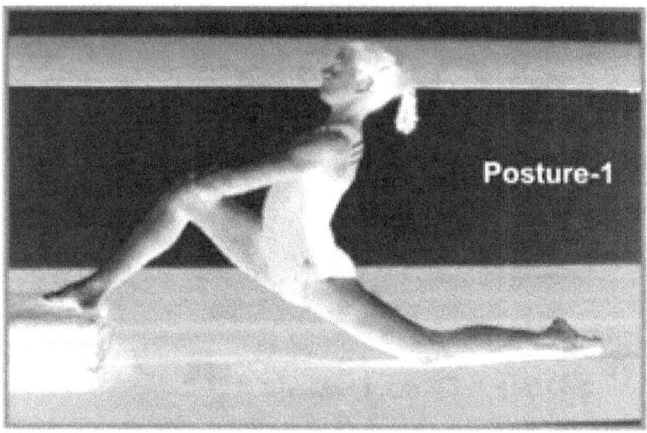

- To imitate the above Advance Stretch, a kneeling stance put one foot in front of you on a mat.

- On the other foot over a step, or some other object about **one foot** or more off the ground.

- Bend your leg to 90 degrees, and place your foot flat on the mat.

- Keeping your hips facing the mat, move the other leg facing backward, bending your knee behind you, until you form a "mini-split" from knee to knee.

- Push your hips forward as much as possible, working towards 180 degrees from knee to knee.

- Keep your chest up and your hands on your front knee.

- Attempt to hold this stretch position for about 30-60 seconds at a time. **Repeat this 3 to 4 times.**

Posture – 2

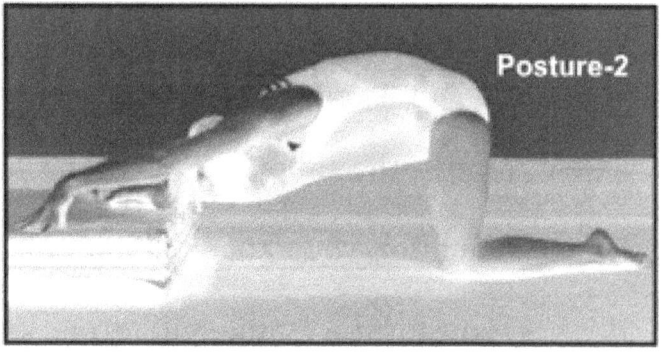

- Put one leg up straight in front of you onto the mat from a kneeling position.

- Move your body back, so only your heel is on the mat.

- Your back leg should be at a 90-degree angle, and your hips should be in a "square" position – they should be facing the mat, not turned one way or the other.

- Keep your front leg straight and lean as forward as possible.

- Attempt to hold this stretch position for 30-60 seconds at a time.

- Repeat 4 to 5 times till you can do it easily and without any pain.

Posture – 3

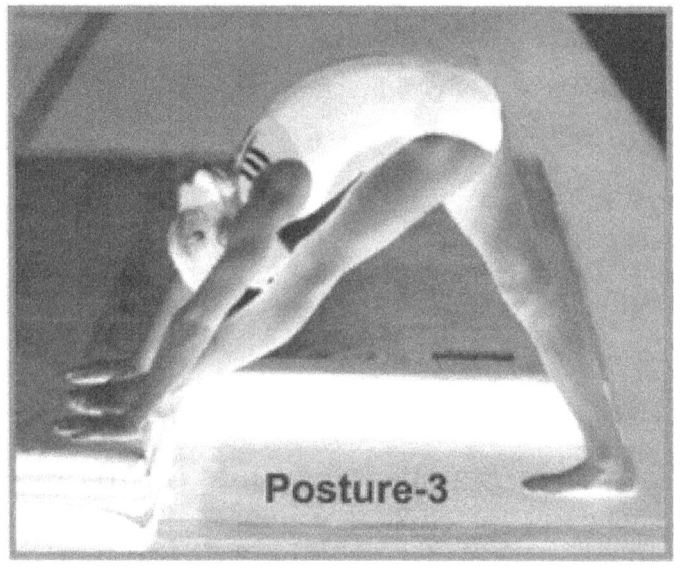

- From a standing position, put one leg on the mat in front of you.

- Keeping both legs straight and your hips square, lean forward as far as possible.

- Your back foot should be placed on the ground and your foot straight or turned slightly out.

- Repeat 4 to 5 times till you can do it easily.

Posture – 4

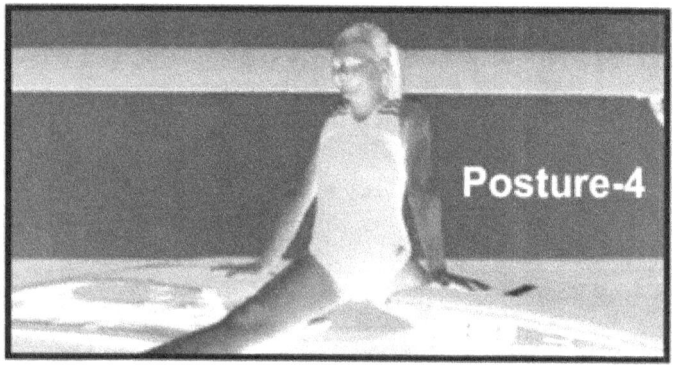

- You should keep your hips in a square position with your body.

- Your torso should be facing straight, and not to the side.

- You have to do it even if squaring your hips means you can't go down as far.

- Both of your legs should be straight and turned slightly outward.

- Your toes are to be kept in a pointed position.

- Your chest should be up, and not leaning forward.

- You can achieve this Posture – 4 with a little trial.

- Do it several times till you can perform this advance stretch quickly and easily.

Posture – 5

- In this Posture – 5, you have to make sure that your hips are square.

- It is best to try doing your split against a wall.

- Your back knee should be almost touching the wall, and your back leg should be bent at a 90-degree angle upward.

- Be sure that your back foot is pointing straight to the ceiling.

- You can also do this stretch with a friend holding your leg and helping you to keep your foot pointing straight up.

- Repeat this Split at least 4 to 5 times till you achieve perfection.

(Remember, you are very close to a perfect Splits).

Posture – 6

- You have already done a square split on the floor in Posture -5. See this position carefully.

- This is just a little advance pose, and just one step away from a perfect split. Now you have to put your foot on the mat. This will ensure your legs are over split or in other words a split more than 180 degrees.

- For even more of a stretch, do your split between two mats or two springboards.

- Repeat this split till your posture is just a mirror image of Posture-6.

Posture – Perfect

This is "THE PERFECT SPLITS!"

Chapter 9 - Tips for 180 - Degree "Side Splits".

We have covered enough illustrative documents by which you can develop the required flexibility for a successful 180 degrees side splits session. However, you must read the documents, refer to Chapter 1 to 8, understand these techniques and try to develop your flexibility to meet the challenges of a Side Splits.

Side Splits requires less flexibility. I can assure you from my years of experience that if you stretch every day, you will likely see a lot of improvement in your flexibility. The Side Split is typically done facing forward with the legs extended out of the side in a 180 Deg. Split.

The Ultimate "7 Steps DAILY Stretching Exercises" to realize your goal of 180 Degree Side Splits

- **Step 1) Jog for 5 Minutes** to warm up your muscles – follow "Chapter -3 – Always warm up first".

- **Step 2) Stand on your feet shoulder-width apart** by pointing your toes slightly out. Bend your right knee. Slide your left leg out until you feel a stretch. Place your hands on the floor in front of you and maintain balance. Hold for 20 seconds. Repeat the same thing on your right leg.

- **Step 3) Stand on your feet with legs together.** Lower your upper body towards your leg – keep your legs straight. Wrap your arms around the back of your legs. Hold this position for 20 seconds. Reach your toes with your hands and hold for 20 seconds. This will stretch your hamstrings.

- **Step 4) Place your feet in a wide "V" Posture.** Lower down your upper body towards the floor, and remain there for at least 20 seconds. Now reach both hands to your left foot and attempt to hold it for about 20 seconds. Similarly, reach both hands to your right foot and hold for 20 seconds.

- **Step 5) Place your feet in a wide "V" Posture.** Twist your torso to the right and then bend your right knee to a 90-degree angle. Keep your left leg straight. Hold the position for about 20 seconds. Repeat on the other side to stretch the hip flexors.

- **Step 6) Sit on the floor with your knees bent** and the bottoms of your feet together. Lean slightly forward with a flat back. Pull your feet towards you until you feel the stretch. Hold for 30 seconds to stretch the gluteal muscles.

- **Step 7) Sit close to a wall.** Bend your knees and then place them on a mat. Slide your knees apart, so your thighs are in a "V" position. Your shins should be flat on the mat. Lean forward and place your forearms flat on the floor. Push your torso back toward the wall behind you. Keep your back flat. Hold for 20 seconds.

Chapter 10 - Contract & Relax

You have gone through a vigorous stretching exercise to achieve a 180 degree or 160 degree Side Splits. Now is the time to relax.

What happens when you stretch?

When you stretch, your nervous system activates the myotatic reflex or muscle contraction in response to stretching within the muscle. This is a stretch reflex – a mechanism of your body's natural defence against muscle tears. Your muscles will react when it feels they have gone too far. The good news is that you can train your reflex to fire much later, thus improving your pre-tensile range of motion, which determines how far you can stretch before your muscles tense up.

Contract and Relax training (CR Training) is an action in which all your muscles will go completely slack and remove all tension to avoid further injury.

Just follow these steps:

- **Step 1) Start your CR Training with the Horse Stance Position.**

One easy way to assume this position is to stand straight up and bend your legs slightly. Place your body in such a way that your hands rest on your waist or hips, and your feet parallel to one another with straight back and knees bent. Now slightly start moving your feet far and farther away from one another such that it puts a stretch on the muscles of the back of your thigh.

If you are not at ease at this position for the first time, use some support to balance your body but remember the support is not to be used to bear your body weight. Keep your knees bent at all times during this "Horse Stance Position," because it is necessary to stress and fatigue your muscles and not your joints. The idea is to lock your knees and thus to sprain the knee-joint. You should feel relaxed.

- **Step 2) Gradually increase the stress on your muscles.**

You can do this by stretching them wide apart in HORSE STANCE POSITION. You will start feeling moderate tension. Remember, we are training your muscles to become habitual of stress and tension. You should not push yourself too hard to feel pain. Do it at ease and take your time. Be patient. You will feel relaxed by practice and over time.

- **Step 3) When you feel the first slight of stress, do this!**

Maintain your position when you feel the first slight of stress. Do not worry if at this point you have only wiggled your feet about a few inches, this is the first stretch, so this is the maximum you can do. While maintaining this position vigorously contract your muscles, enough that your legs start trembling. It happens because you are trying to move your legs close to one another and yet contracting them. Your legs at this point will look like two sharp ends of scissors.

HOLD YOUR CONTRACTION FOR AT LEAST 30 SECS AND TIME IT USING A STOPWATCH. DO NOT TOUCH THE FLOOR OR USE A SUPPORT TO BEAR YOUR WEIGHT. FOCUS THE WEIGHT ON YOUR LEGS.

OBSERVE: *At this point, your hands SHOULD NOT be on your knees, knees should be BENT and hips ROLLED. The level of ease of the next stretch depends on the duration of the first intense contraction.*

- **Step 4) Deeper Stretches**

After the first intense contraction maintain the posture for another 30 seconds and let your muscles relax. Perform a deeper stretch by moving your legs further apart to keep tension on your muscles.

This is the second contraction. Now after the second stress, STOP & CONTRACT AGAIN for another 30 seconds. When this contraction is over, RELAX your muscles and go for one more profound and intense STRETCH.

Now the third time when you are doing a stretch, and you can feel a CONTRACTION, hold this position for the same time span. This is the 3rd contraction. When this contraction is over bring the legs close to one another, shake them around, walk around and relax for 3-4 minutes. You will feel much better. Are you a bit confused?

- Let us **summarize the 4 Steps**:

THREE INTENSE CONTRACTIONS EACH HAVING DURATION OF 30 SECONDS MAKES ONE COMPLETE SET OF CONTRACTIONS.

- Align your body in horse stance position, move your feet apart causing your muscles to feel tension, STOP and CONTRACT for 30 seconds.

- Hold this contraction.

- Repeat this process twice till the third contraction is approached creating a DEEPER STRETCH.

- Stop pulling and RELAX.

RECOVERY TIME:

3-4 minutes, but don't stress your body this time can surely vary from person to person. So if you need more time to loosen up your muscles or relax, take that time because we don't want you to be uninspired by your progress.

- **Step 5) Complete a stretching session.**

  You can accomplish this by performing THREE TO FIVE TOTAL SETS OF CONTRACTIONS.

- **Step 6) Last Intense Contraction.**

  This Step is a modification of the last contraction and a little hard to achieve. This will also consume more time.

  Hold the very **LAST INTENSE CONTRACTION** for an exceptionally long time-span that is from **60-90** seconds. It is because of this duration that the last step is necessary for TREMENDOUS FINAL RESULTS because it is a strenuous task to accumulate the contraction for such an extended period of time.

Now carefully walk out of this stance and relax and loosen your muscles.

As you find yourself progressing with the stretching techniques rather than just dropping the method totally and giving it a fresh start every time, you should instead go with MINI CONTRACTIONS midway through the stretches.

1. Walk your feet apart until you have reached a few inches

2. Stop

3. Perform mini contractions for 3-5 seconds

4. Again walk your feet apart until you have reached a few more inches

5. Stop again

6. Perform mini contractions AGAIN for 3-5 seconds

7. REPEAT this whole process one more time

8. Keep doing it until you start feeling STRESS on your thighs

9. After feeling the pressure, do the EXTREME 30 seconds CONTRACTION.

Yes, you are done! You have successfully ELONGATED your muscles by REPEATED ISOMETRIC CONTRACTIONS.

Know the following truth about Relaxed Stretches:

- You can do Relaxed Stretches anytime, anywhere, and without any warm up.

- You must be patient while doing Relax Stretches.

- Never bounce in any stretch.

- Do Relax Stretches at the very end of the workouts.

- The optional frequency for Relax Stretches is once every day.

- Rotate your pelvis to prevent pain occurring at the top of your pelvis.

- Unlike dynamic stretching, it does not cause fatigue, which means even after an intense workout you can still, do a thorough stretching routine.

- It can be done any time of the day with or without a warm-up.

- It can be done by anyone regardless of his or her fitness level.

- It is the most enjoyable form of stretching and can leave you feeling completely relaxed.

At this point try to have 5 minutes for yourself to think about your expectations and how it is changing you now and in the future. We will now add some important documents relevant to "SPLITS METHOD."

Well, I feel that it is necessary to answer some relevant questions often asked by participants.

Chapter 11 - Practice Splits Every Day

When you do the splits, you spread your legs at right angles to your torso. As I mentioned several times before, to do the splits, you have to be quite flexible.

Your feet work best when your legs are spread against a flat surface. While some people are naturally more flexible than others, you can improve your flexibility with regular practice.

Practice the splits daily to see improvement

If you are still not able to do a full splits, practice stretching daily, and you will find you can spread your legs a bit farther each day – eventually to successful full splits.

- **Step 1):** Warm up your muscles by walking, jogging or performing exercises as outlined in Chapter - 4 – "Always warm up first" – Page – 15, or you may resort to some other cardiovascular exercise. If you do not properly warm up before attempting the splits, you may hurt yourself.

- **Step 2):** Choose which leg will be in front. Most people have more flexibility on one side. Find out your flexibility by trial.

- **Step 3):** Place one foot forward and the other behind you.

- **Step 4):** Slide your to away. You will slowly inch down toward the floor.

- **Step 5):** Use your arms to stabilize your body, as you get closer to the floor. Your hands should be placed on the floor for support.

- **Step 6):** Stop sliding when you feel discomfort in your legs. Do not continue if you feel pain. If you do, you may pull a muscle.

- **Step 7):** Remain in the splits position for a few minutes. This will help your muscles to become accustomed to the pose.

- **Step 8):** Practice the splits every day. You'll find you can get closer to full splits every time you practice.

You must record your daily progress, and hopefully, you will do the full sooner than you think! :)

Chapter 12 - Leg Stretches

I've purposely made sure to devote an entire Chapter on Leg Stretches. You may ask – why? Leg stretches are a critical factor of Side Splits, lower back health, and comfort. When the muscles of the legs become tight and short (it often happens due to sitting for long periods of time), they can fix the position of the pelvis preventing casual movement. When the pelvis is in a fixed position, the lower back can become strained, as it tries to compensate for movement.

What should be your goal be while performing Leg Stretches?

Your goal should be to lengthen the adductor muscles so that they do not prevent the natural movement of your pelvis during splits. Look at the pictures below.

Basic Leg Stretches Exercise

Gently ease down into a side splits. It's not important how far you're able to go. What's important is that you feel a comfortable stretch. Again, if you push your muscles too hard, they will rebel.

If you are not able to get your hands on the floor, use something else for support. See the picture on the next page.

If the above piece is not high enough for you, you may use a chair or even a countertop. Make yourself comfortable in this position, and then gently rock back and forth so that you will feel a rhythmic increase or decrease of the leg stretch. Don't spend longer than 30 seconds. It is best to come out and repeat it.

Leg Stretches for the Hamstrings:

To ensure the comfort of the lower back and to prevent the progression of sciatica symptoms the hamstrings must undergo a regular stretch session.

Those who occupy a sitting position for much of the day are particularly prone to tight, short hamstrings. Tight hamstrings, like tight adductors, can exert a powerful immobilizing effect on the pelvis, which puts a strain on the lower back.

Lie on your back with one leg straight out on the floor. Grasp the back of the thigh of the other leg and straighten toward the ceiling. Don't worry if your leg doesn't straighten all the way! What's important is that you straighten as far as you're able to without too much strain, hold for just 2 seconds, then release allowing the knee to bend completely. Now repeat 10 times.

Two things likely distinguish this stretch from hamstring stretches you've done in the past:

> 1. You're not trying to stretch the hamstrings while holding up your body weight such as you would in a standing position
>
> 2. You're not holding the stretch for longer than 2 seconds. Instead, you're repeating the stretch 10 times.

For very tight hamstrings I have found that this strategy is far more effective than static stretching in which the stretch is held for, say, 30 seconds. For those who wish to get a deeper stretch reach up higher on the leg during the lengthening phase as shown in the picture here.

See the picture above. You can reach for the deepest stretch for the foot during lengthening process as shown in the picture here.

Leg Stretches for the Quadriceps:

My goal is to lengthen the quadriceps muscles (the front of the upper thigh) so that they do not pull the pelvis into an anterior torque, which can strain the lower back.

The Kneeling Version: Begin in the supported position as shown in the picture above. Now bend forward while retaining a hold on the ankle so that you feel a deepening of the stretch into the quadriceps. Hold no longer that 1-2 seconds then straighten up again. Repeat 4-6 times, each time attempting to sink a little deeper into the stretch.

Switch legs and repeat this sequence. See the picture below:

The Side-lying Version:

Begin in the side-lying position shown in the next page the image.

Now reach back with the left knee while stabilizing the left ankle and hold for no longer than **1-2 seconds** (Do not try to hold longer as it develops fatigue).

Repeat reaching back, feeling the quadriceps stretch for just 1-2 seconds, and then returning to the starting position. Repeat 4-6 times.

Repeat entire sequence on the other side as shown in the picture.

How to Improve Your Flexibility Safety During Splits.

Again, I cannot repeat this enough times. You should not make the common mistake of trying to push too hard during stretches. While doing so, you will risk tearing your muscle fibers. Muscles have a protective response called "Stretch Reflex" which makes the muscle contract during hard stretches. Thus pushing too hard has a detrimental effect. You will not get the desired result and at the same time risk tearing your muscles. So, the best technique is to do stretches gently and gradually over an extended period of time.

Bonus Chapter: Video Stretching Tutorial

http://

www.hmwpublishing.com/

splitsbonus

*Please DO NOT share this video. This is an unlisted video URL link and is intended to be viewed by customers who purchased this book only. Thank you.

Final Words

Thank you again for purchasing this book!

I really hope this book is able to help you.

The next step is for you to join our email newsletter to receive updates on any upcoming new book releases or promotions. You can sign-up for free, and as a bonus, you will receive a free gift. Our "*Health & Fitness Mistakes You Don't Know You're Making*" book! This book has been written to demystify, expose the top do's and don'ts and to finally equip you with the information you need to get in the best shape of your life. Due to the overwhelming amount of mis-information and lies told by magazines and self-proclaimed "gurus", it's becoming harder and harder to get reliable information to get in shape. As opposed to having to go through dozens of biased, unreliable and untrustworthy sources to get your health & fitness information. Everything you need to help you has been broken down in this book for you to easily follow and to immediately get results to achieve your desired fitness goals in the shortest amount of time.

Once again, to join our free email newsletter and to receive a free copy of this valuable book, please visit the link and signup now:

www.hmwpublishing.com/gift

Finally, if you enjoyed this book, then I would like to ask you for a favor, would you be kind enough to leave a review for this book? It would be greatly appreciated!

Thank you and good luck in your journey!

About the Co-Author

My name is George Kaplo; I'm a certified personal trainer from Montreal, Canada. I'll start off by saying I'm not the biggest guy you will ever meet and this has never really been my goal. In fact, I started working out to overcome my biggest insecurity when I was younger, which was my self-confidence. This was due to my height measuring only 5 foot 5 inches (168cm), it pushed me down to attempt anything I ever wanted to achieve in life. You may be going through some challenges right now, or you may simply want to get fit, and I can certainly relate.

For me personally, I was always kind of interested in the

health & fitness world and wanted to gain some muscle due to the numerous bullying in my teenage years about my height and my overweight body. I figured I couldn't do anything about my height, but I sure can do something about how my body looked like. This was the beginning of my transformation journey. I had no idea where to start, but I just got started. I felt worried and afraid at times that other people would make fun of me for doing the exercises the wrong way. I always wished I had a friend that was next to me who was knowledgeable enough to help me get started and "show me the ropes."

After a lot of work, studying and countless trial and errors. Some people began to notice how I was getting more fit and how I was starting to form a keen interest in the topic. This led many friends and new faces to come to me and ask me for fitness advice. At first, it seemed odd when people asked me to help them get in shape. But what kept me going is when they started to see changes in their own body and told me it's the first time that they saw real results! From there, more people kept coming to me, and it made me realize after so much reading and studying in this field that it did help me but it also allowed me to help others. I'm now a fully certified personal trainer and have trained numerous clients to date who have achieved amazing results.

Today, my brother Alex Kaplo (also a Certified Personal Trainer) and I own & operate this publishing venture, where we bring passionate and expert authors to write about health and fitness topics. We also run an online fitness website "HelpMeWorkout.com" and I would love to connect with by inviting you to visit the website on the following page and signing up to our e-mail newsletter (you will even get a free book).

Last but not least, if you are in the position I was once in and you want some guidance, don't hesitate and ask... I'll be there to help you out!

Your friend and coach,

George Kaplo

Certified Personal Trainer

Download another book for Free

I want to thank you for purchasing this book and offer you another book (just as long and valuable as this book), "Health & Fitness Mistakes You Don't Know You're Making", completely free.

Visit the link below to signup and receive it:

www.hmwpublishing.com/gift

In this book, I will break down the most common health & fitness mistakes, you are probably committing right now, and I will reveal how you can easily get in the best shape of your life!

In addition to this valuable gift, you will also have an opportunity to get our new books for free, enter giveaways, and receive other valuable emails from me. Again, visit the link to sign up:

www.hmwpublishing.com/gift

Copyright 2017 by HMW Publishing - All Rights Reserved.

This document by HMW Publishing owned by the A&G Direct Inc company, is geared towards providing exact and reliable information in regards to the topic and issue covered. The publication is sold with the idea that the publisher is not required to render accounting, officially permitted, or otherwise, qualified services. If advice is necessary, legal or professional, a practiced individual in the profession should be ordered.

From a Declaration of Principles which was accepted and approved equally by a Committee of the American Bar Association and a Committee of Publishers and Associations.

In no way is it legal to reproduce, duplicate, or transmit any part of this document in either electronic means or in printed format. Recording of this publication is strictly prohibited, and any storage of this document is not allowed unless with written permission from the publisher. All rights reserved.

The information provided herein is stated to be truthful and consistent, in that any liability, in terms of inattention or otherwise, by any usage or abuse of any policies, processes, or directions contained within is the solitary and utter responsibility of the recipient reader. Under no circumstances will any legal responsibility or blame be held against the publisher for any reparation, damages, or monetary loss due to the information herein, either directly or indirectly.

The information herein is offered for informational purposes solely, and is universal as so. The presentation of the information is without contract or any type of guarantee assurance.

The trademarks that are used are without any consent, and the publication of the trademark is without permission or backing by the trademark owner. All trademarks and brands within this book are for clarifying purposes only and are the owned by the owners themselves, not affiliated with this document.

For more great books visit:

HMWPublishing.com

www.ingramcontent.com/pod-product-compliance
Lightning Source LLC
Chambersburg PA
CBHW071852070526
44583CB00016B/1656